Around the World

Megan Higgins

WINDMILL BOOKS

Published in 2020 by Windmill Books,
an Imprint of Rosen Publishing
29 East 21st Street, New York, NY 10010

Cataloging-in-Publication Data

Names: Higgins, Megan.
Title: Around the world / Megan Higgins.
Description: New York : Windmill Books, 2020. | Series: Spot-a-thon
Identifiers: ISBN 9781725394582 (pbk.) | ISBN 9781725394605 (library bound) |
ISBN 9781725394599 (6 pack)
Subjects: LCSH: Picture puzzles--Juvenile literature.
Classification: LCC GV1507.P47 H544 2020 | DDC 793.73--dc23

Manufactured in the United States of America

CPSIA Compliance Information: Batch BW20WM: For Further Information contact Rosen Publishing,
New York, New York at 1-800-237-9932

CONTENTS

Mountain Mayhem	4	Pitch Perfect	18
Airport Adventures	6	Bat and Ball	19
Takeoff!	7	New York City	20
Trick or Treat!	8	Light of Liberty	21
Pumpkin Faces	9	Mighty Moose	22
Rudolf the Reindeer	10	Sun Fun	23
Spot the Lynx!	11	All Aboard!	24
Boat Trip	12	Gone Surfing!	26
Into India	14	Blastoff!	27
Elegant Elephants	15	Downhill Dashers	28
Crazy Crocs	16	Lost in Space	29
Playtime	17	Answers	30

Step inside a world of fun puzzles!

For some puzzles, you need to spot the differences between two pictures. For others, you need to find the odd one out. You'll find all the answers at the back of the book. Turn the page to get started!

MOUNTAIN MAYHEM

Take a lift to the top of the mountain.
When you get to the bottom, spot ten differences!

AIRPORT ADVENTURES

Where's the stuffed rabbit?

TAKEOFF!

Which hot-air balloon has a passenger waving?

TRICK OR TREAT!

Find two white pumpkins!

PUMPKIN FACES

Find the pumpkin with three eyes.

RUDOLF THE REINDEER

Which reindeer has a red collar around its neck?

SPOT THE LYNX!

Find the lynx with more spots than the rest.

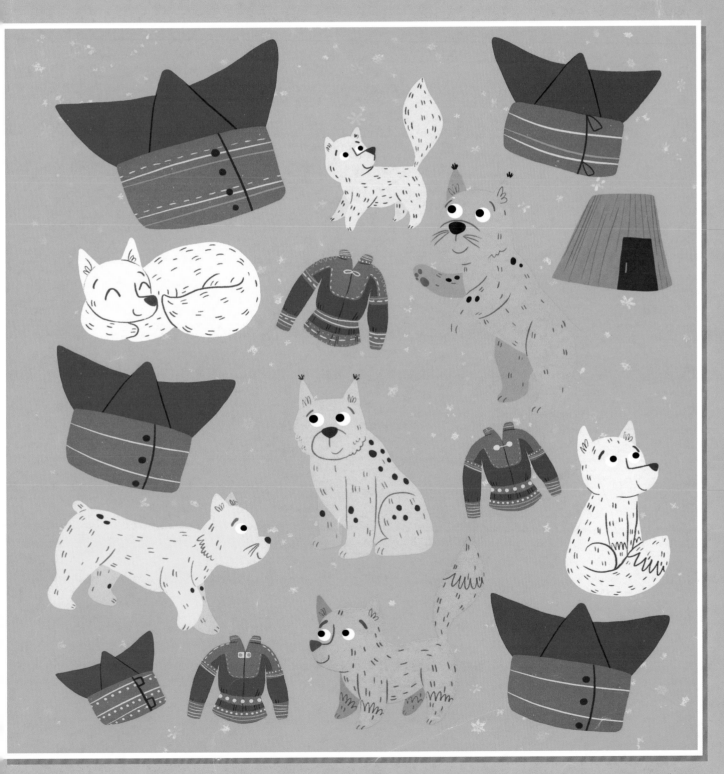

BOAT TRIP

Take a boat trip around the island.
On the way, spot ten differences!

INTO INDIA

Which elephant is about to eat a banana?

ELEGANT ELEPHANTS

Which two elephants are exactly the same?

CRAZY CROCS

Which two crocodiles are identical?

PLAYTIME

Find three kids wearing orange T-shirts.

PITCH PERFECT

Who is bouncing a red basketball?

BAT AND BALL

Which bowling ball has an extra hole?

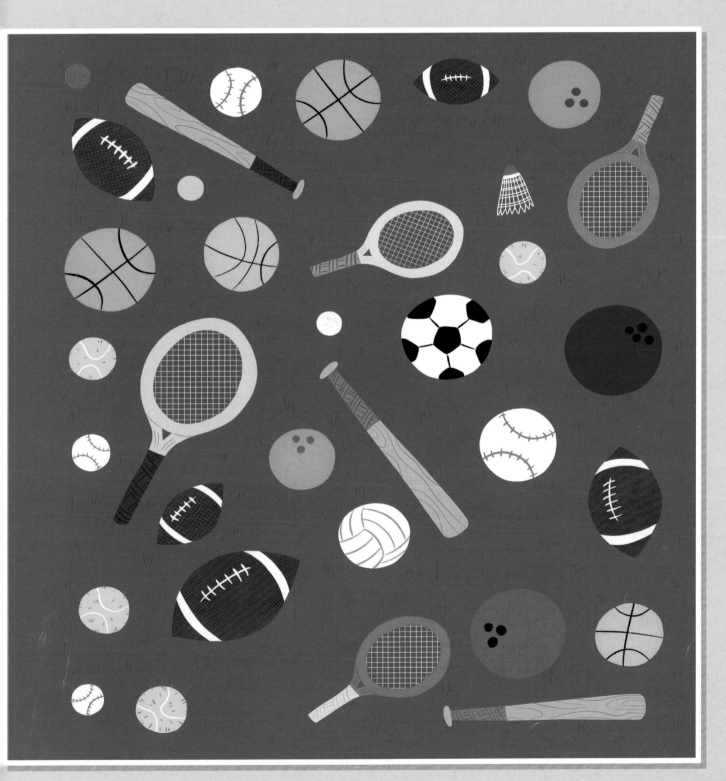

NEW YORK CITY

Which is the tallest building?

LIGHT OF LIBERTY

Which Statue of Liberty is holding a teddy bear?

MIGHTY MOOSE

Which two of these moose are exactly alike?

SUN FUN

Find the green parrot.

ALL ABOARD!

Climb aboard the airplane. When you're sitting comfortably, spot ten differences!

GONE SURFING!

Which windsurfer is wearing a red T-shirt?

BLASTOFF!

Spot the rocket with an alien inside it.

DOWNHILL DASHERS

Which of these snowboarders is different than the others?

LOST IN SPACE

Find three yellow stars.

ANSWERS

Page 4-5 Mountain Mayhem

Page 6 Airport Adventures

Page 7 Takeoff!

Page 8 Trick or Treat!

Page 9 Pumpkin Faces

Page 10 Rudolf the Reindeer

Page 11 Spot the Lynx!

Page 12-13 Boat Trip

Page 14 Into India

Page 15 Elegant Elephants

Page 16 Crazy Crocs

Page 17 Playtime

Page 18 Pitch Perfect

Page 19 Bat and Ball

Page 20 New York City

Page 21 Light of Liberty

Page 22 Mighty Moose

Page 23 Sun Fun

31

Page 24-25 All Aboard!

Page 26 Gone Surfing!

Page 27 Blastoff!

Page 28 Downhill Dashers

Page 29 Lost in Space